# Pat Sat

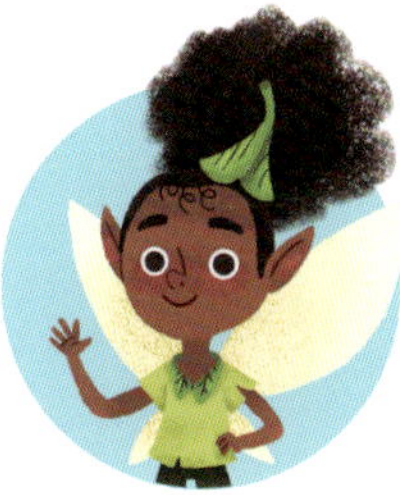

Written by
Stephen Rickard

Illustrated by
Ana Sebastián

Ransom

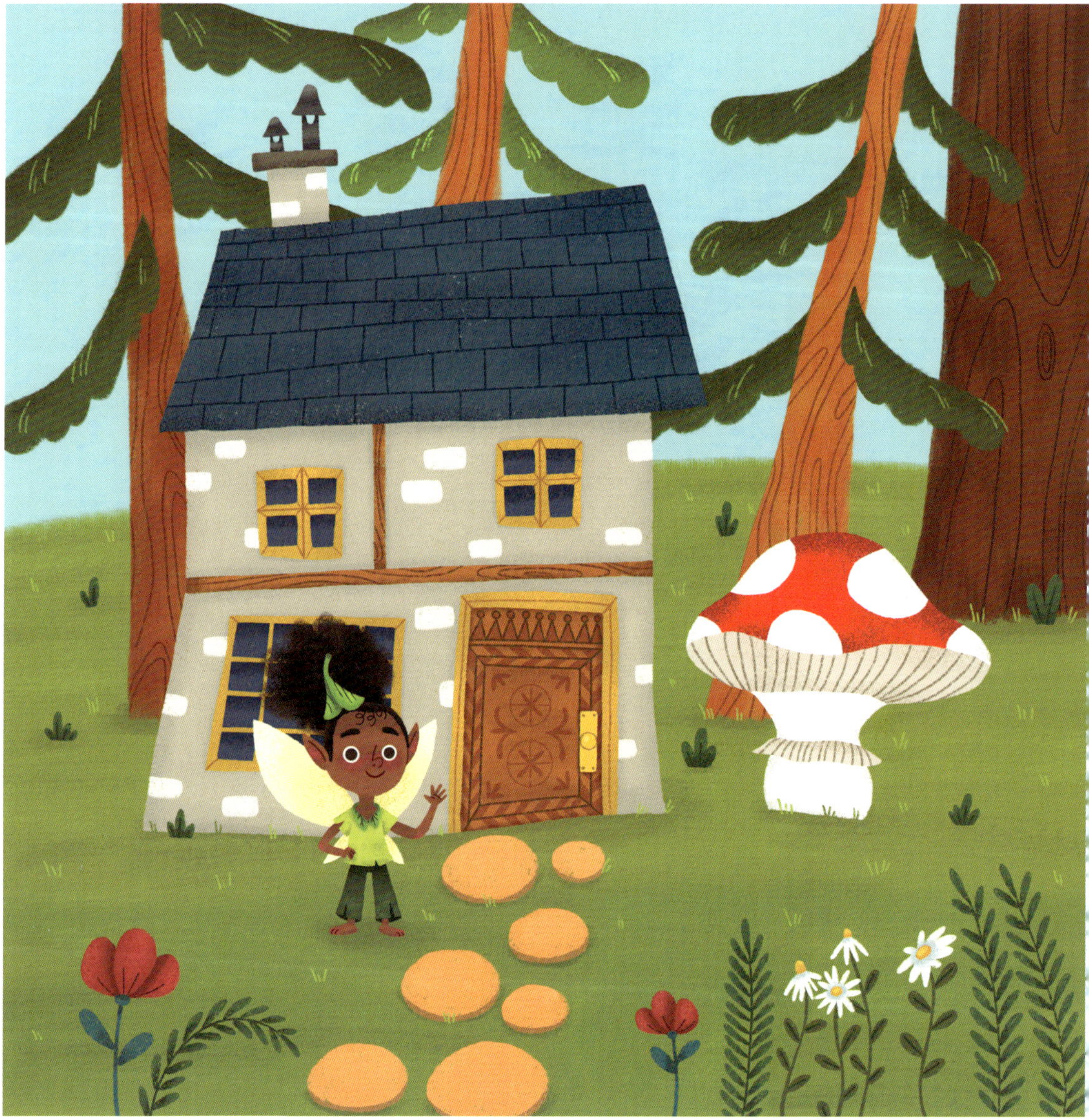

Pat.

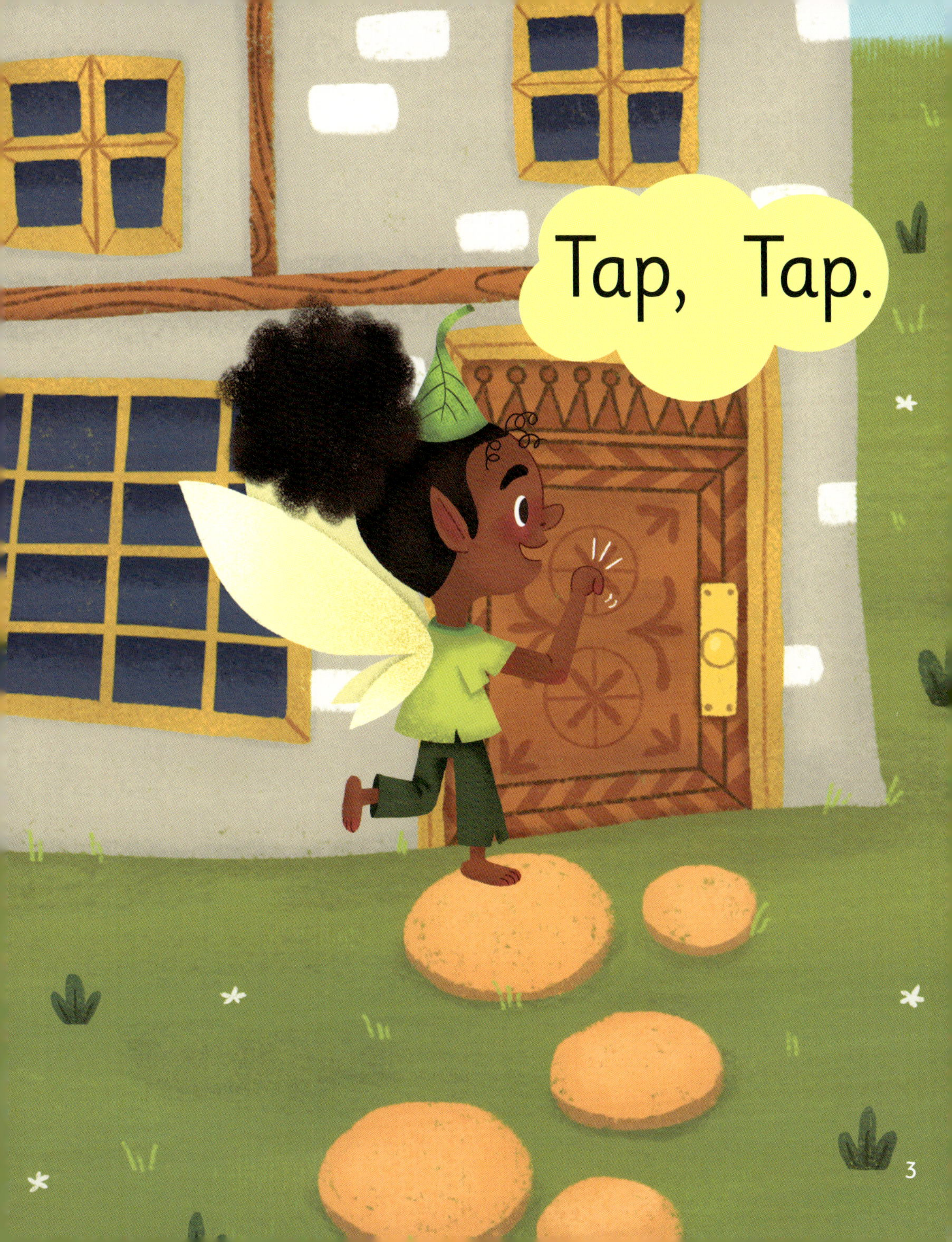
Tap, Tap.

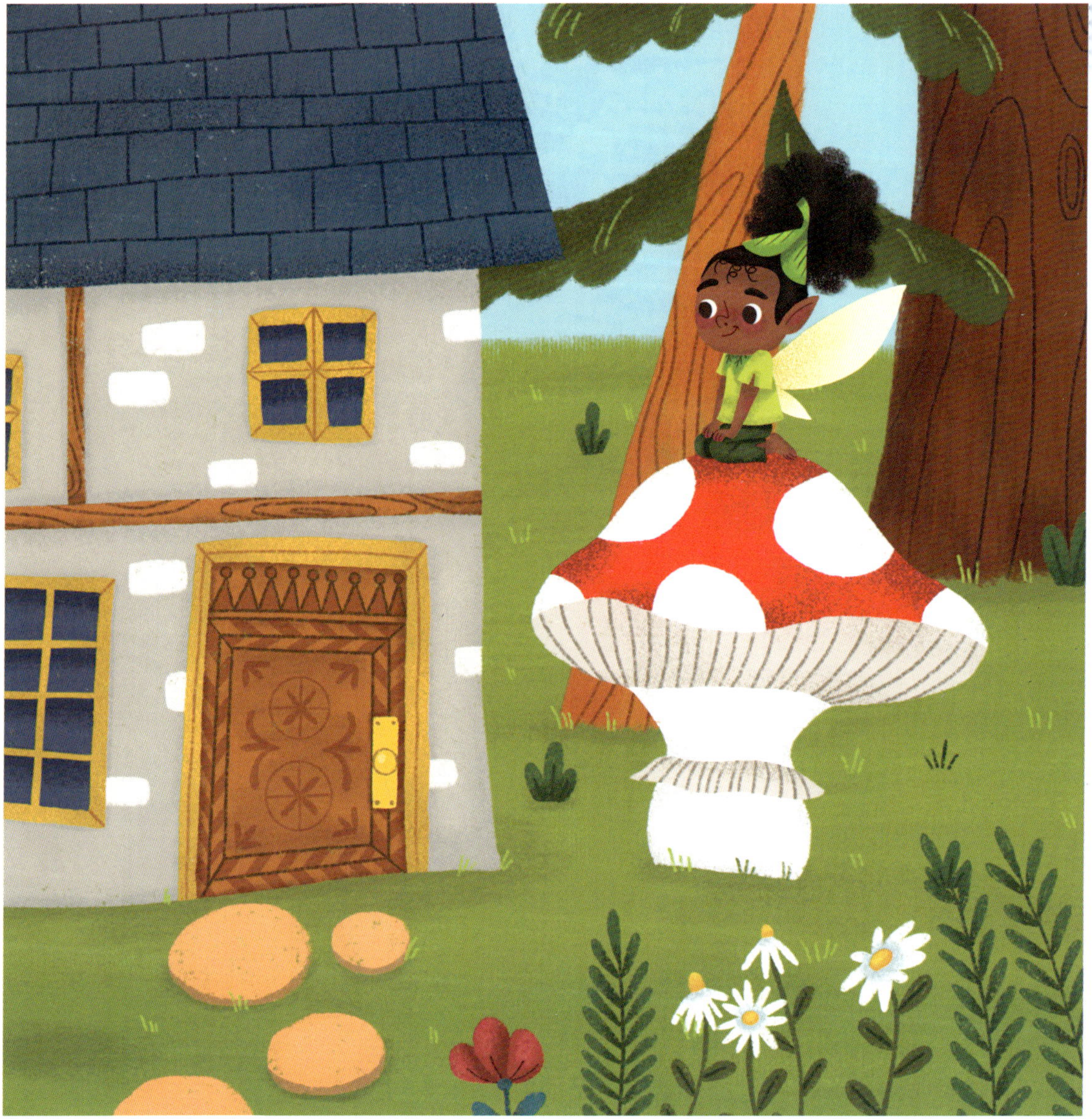

Pat sat.

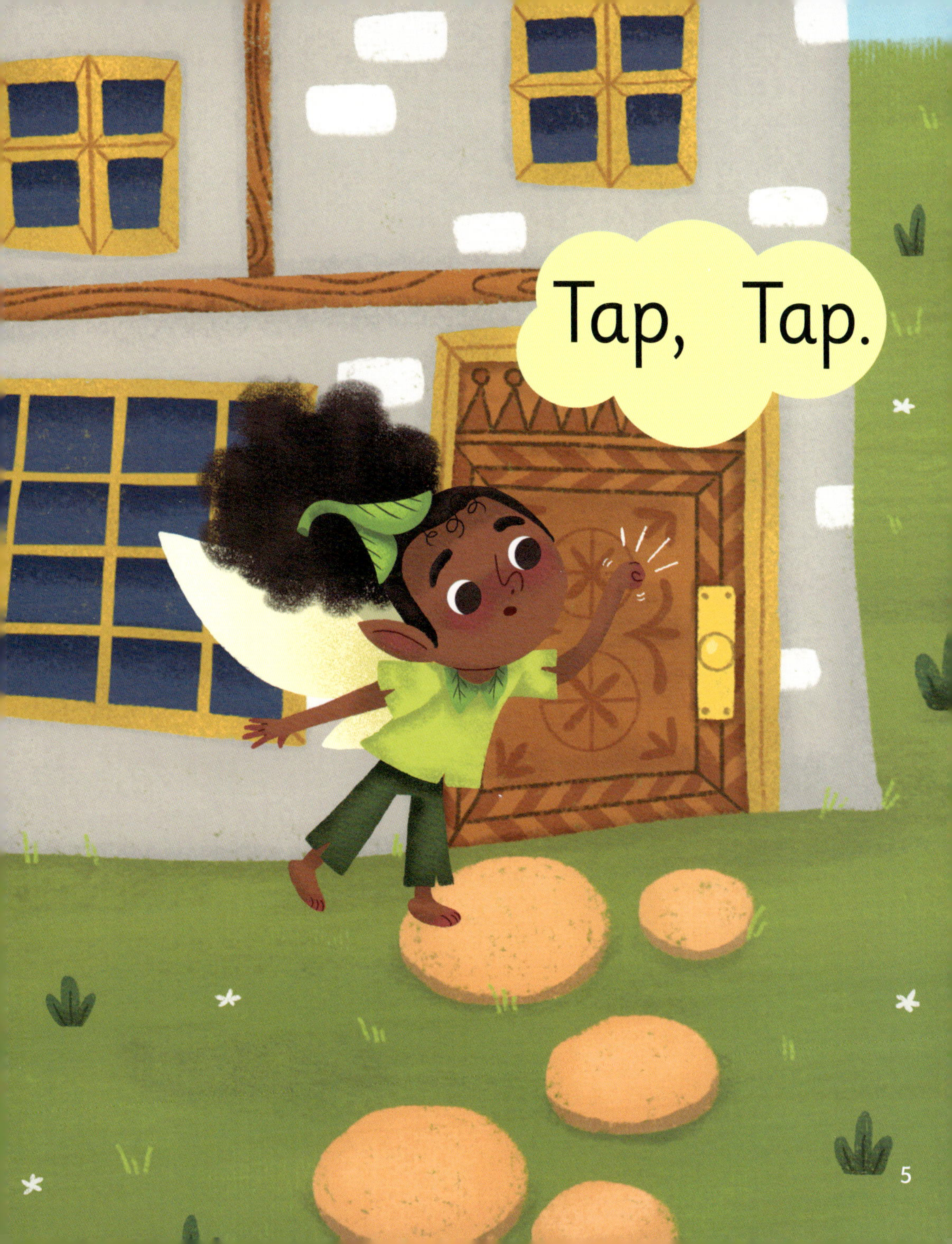
Tap, Tap.

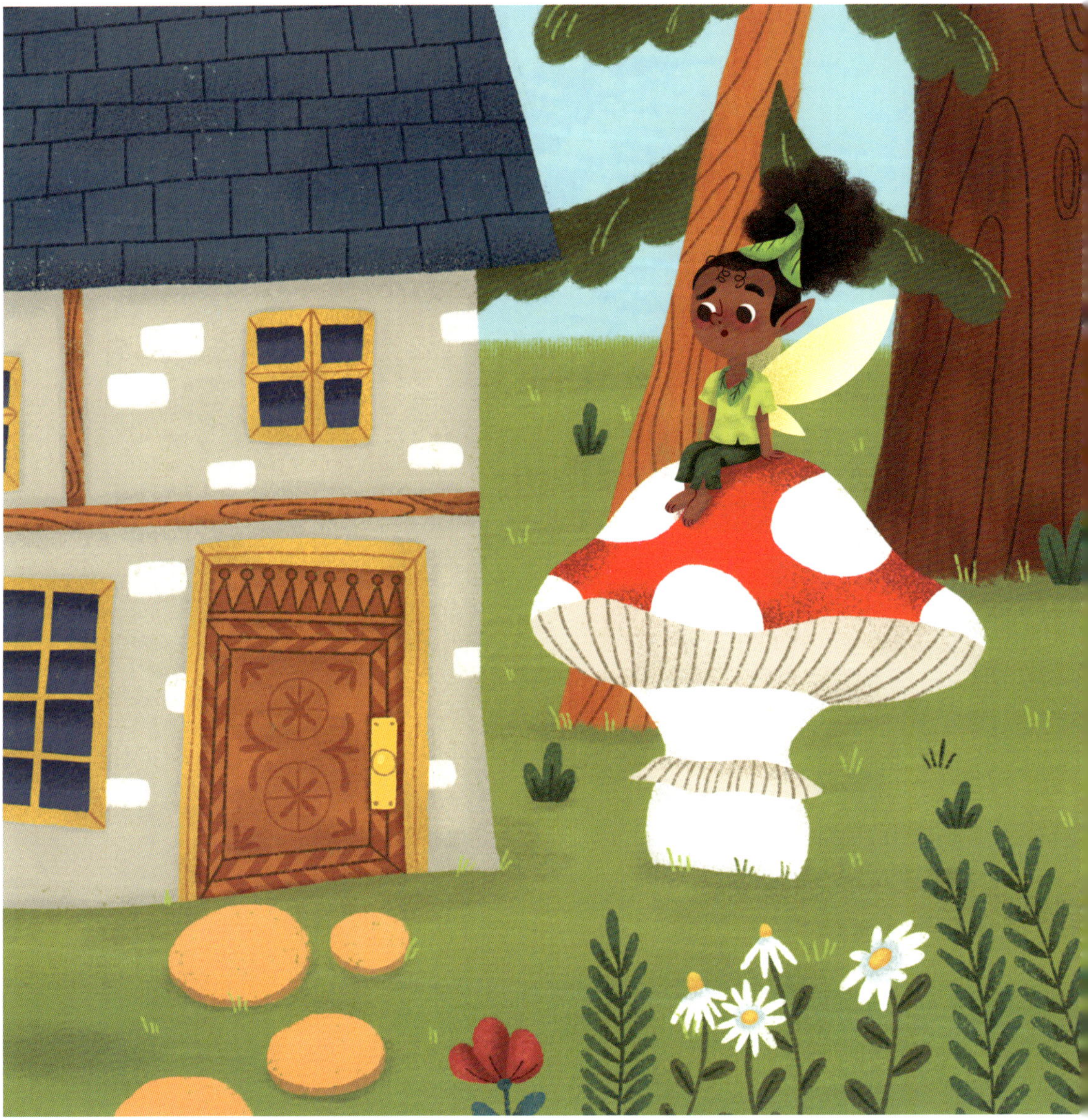

Pat sat.

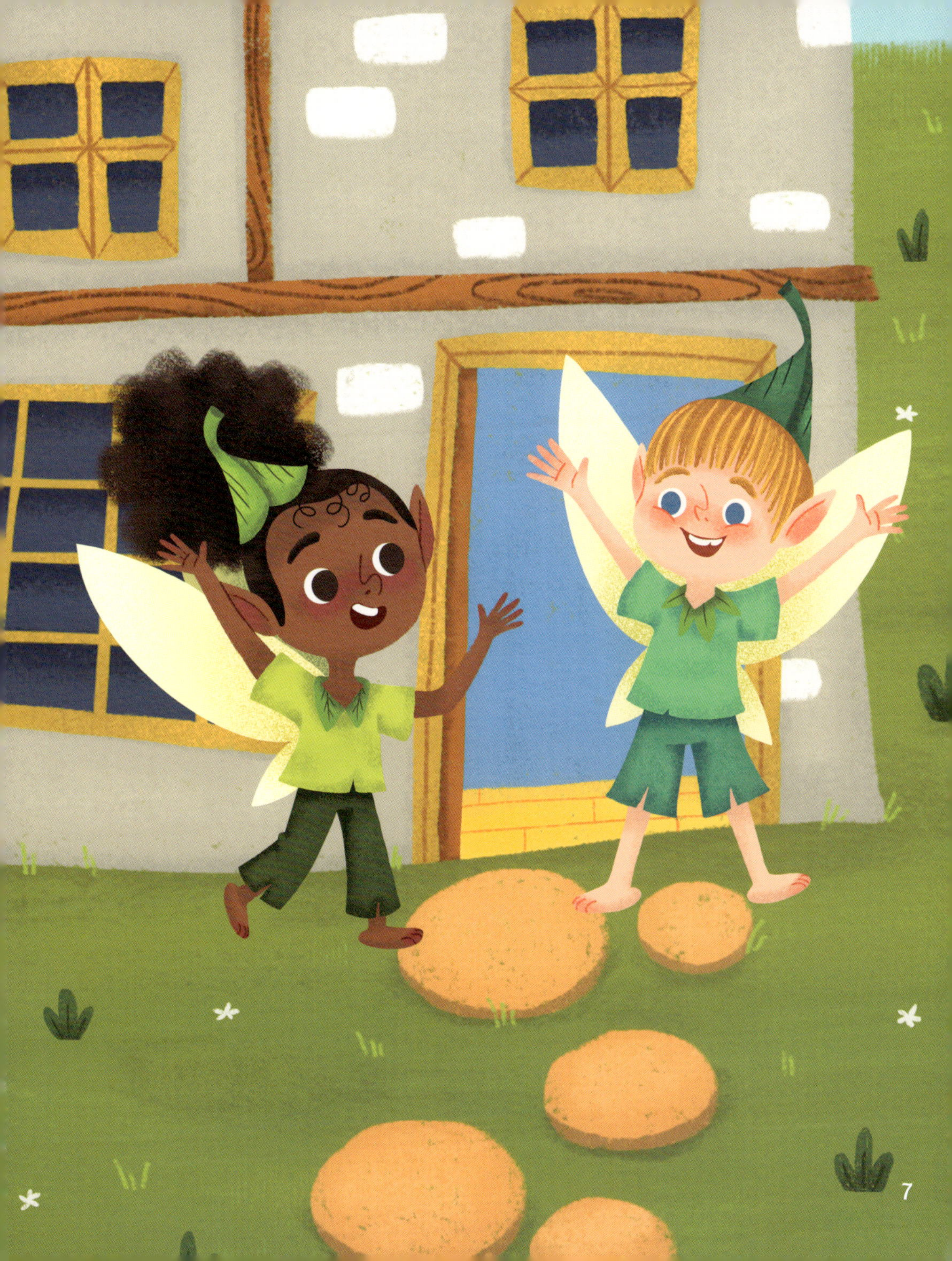

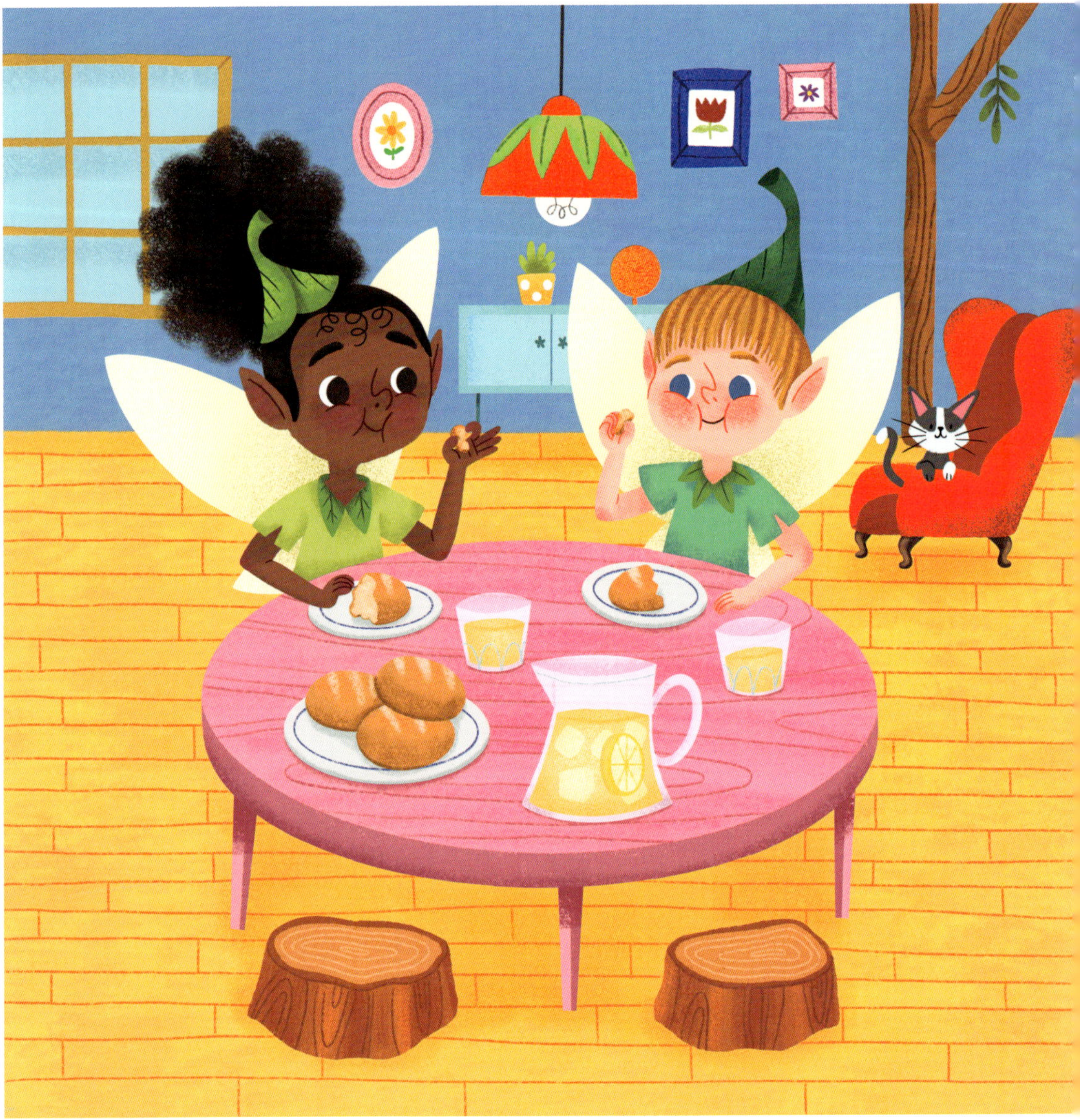

Pat sat.